AF326590

Amandas Traum
Amanda's Dream

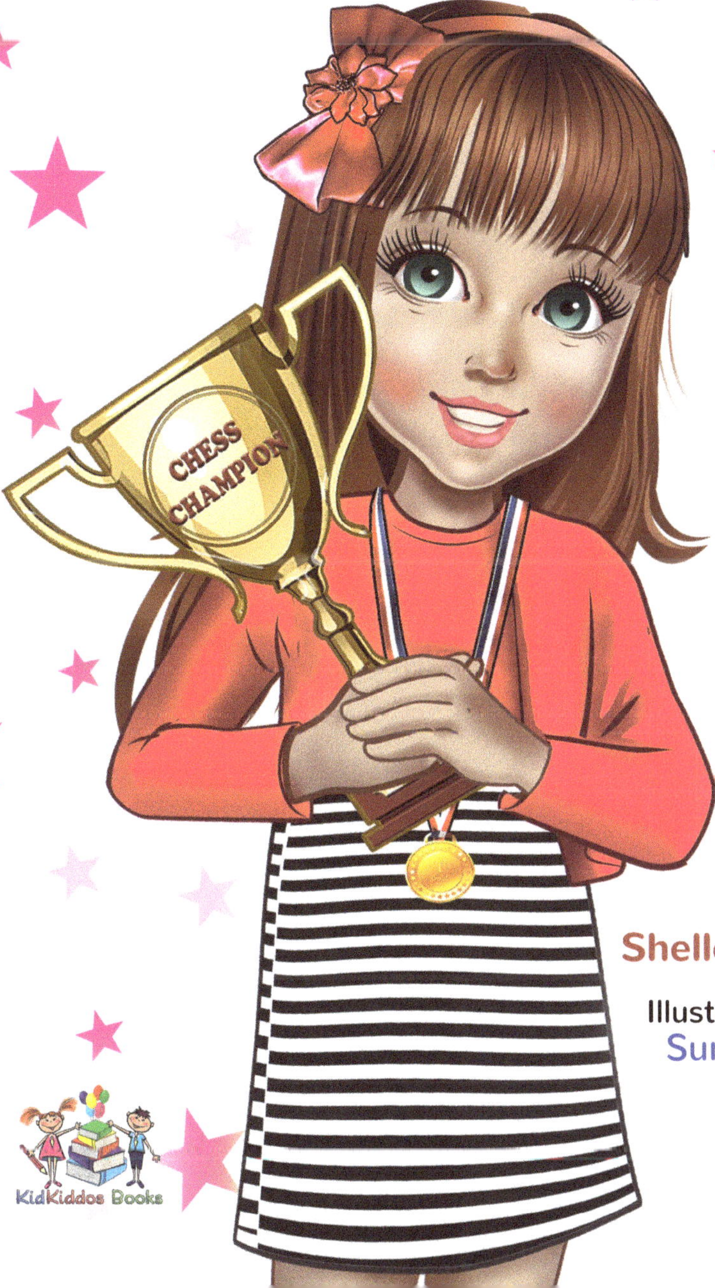

Shelley Admont

Illustrationen von
Sumana Roy

www.kidkiddos.com
Copyright ©2013 by S.A. Publishing ©2017 by KidKiddos Books Ltd.
support@kidkiddos.com

First edition, 2020

Aus dem Englischen übersetzt von Tess Parthum
Translated from English by Tess Parthum
Deutsche Überarbeitung von Veronika Strauß
German editing by Veronika Strauss

Library and Archives Canada Cataloguing in Publication
Amanda´s Dream (German English Bilingual Edition)/ Shelley Admont
ISBN: 978-1-5259-2042-4 paperback
ISBN: 978-1-5259-2043-1 hardcover
ISBN: 978-1-5259-2041-7 eBook

Please note that the German and English versions of the story have been written to be as close as possible. However, in some cases they differ in order to accommodate nuances and fluidity of each language.

One day, Amanda was sitting on a bench in the park and reading her favorite book.

Out of nowhere, a woman appeared. She wore a beautiful pink dress, and had wavy, flowing locks of hair and big, glowing blue eyes.

"Hello, Amanda," said the woman as she approached the bench. "Why are you sad?"

"I'm not sad," answered Amanda. "I just don't feel like smiling."

"Are you sure? You seem upset," the strange woman replied.

4

Amanda entschied, dass sie mit jemandem reden musste. Sie erzählte der Frau, wie unglücklich sie war. Als Amanda atemlos all ihre Gefühle nur so aussprudelte, begann sie zu weinen.

Amanda decided that she had to talk to someone. She told the woman how unhappy she was. As Amanda breathlessly spilled out all her emotions, she began to cry.

Suddenly, Amanda stopped crying, looked at the strange woman and asked, "Who are you and how do you know my name?"

"I'm a dream fairy," the woman said. "I'm here to help you."

Amanda listened carefully. "You just need a dream—a goal," the fairy continued.

"I know! I really want one. All my friends have a dream," Amanda said with excitement, "and you know what? Their dreams come true."

6

„Danny träumte davon, Fahrrad zu fahren, und letzte Woche hat er ganz allein gelernt zu fahren."
"Danny dreamed of riding a bike, and last week he learned to ride all by himself."

„Lillian träumte davon, Balletttänzerin zu werden, und jetzt hat sie Tanzunterricht und tanzt in verschiedenen Aufführungen."
"Lillian dreamed of being a ballet dancer, and now she has dance lessons and dances in different shows."

„Ich möchte wirklich, dass auch irgendein Traum für mich in Erfüllung geht. Ich weiß nur nicht, wie man einen bekommt."
"I really want to have some kind of dream come true, too. I just don't know how to get one."

„Ein Traum ist nichts, was dir gegeben werden kann", sagte die Traumfee. „Du musst einen in deinem Herzen tragen. Keine Sorge, es ist nicht so schwer, wie es klingt. Ich kann dir helfen."

"A dream isn't something that can be given to you," said the dream fairy. "You need to have one inside your heart. Don't worry, it isn't as hard as it sounds. I can help you."

Amanda looked up at her and wiped away her tears.
She felt much better now.

"All you have to do is go home and think about what
you want," continued the fairy. "Write down all your
favorite things to do and what you love about them."

Danach verschwand sie, als wäre sie gar nie dagewesen.
After that, she disappeared as if she had never been there at all.

Was möchte ich? Ich weiß, ich will ganz viele Süßigkeiten, dachte Amanda auf dem Weg nach Hause. Nein, warum brauche ich ganz viele Süßigkeiten? Ich werde ein paar essen und dann keine mehr wollen.
What do I want? I know, I want a lot of candy, thought Amanda on her way home. *No, why do I need a lot of candy? I'll eat a little and then not want any more.*

Ich will ganz viele verschieden Puppen, dachte sie, aber dann änderte sie ihre Meinung wieder. Nein, ich brauche nicht ganz viele Puppen. Ich habe schon genug.
I want a lot of dolls of all different kinds, she thought, but then changed her mind again. *No, I don't need a lot of dolls. I have enough already.*

„Also, was will ich?", Amanda überlegte angestrengt weiter, was ihr Traum sein könnte. Vielleicht ein süßer, kleiner Hund?

So what do I want? Amanda continued to think hard about what her dream could be. *Maybe a cute little dog?*

‚Nein, es wäre besser, neue Buntstifte oder schöne Ohrringe zu haben. Oder vielleicht will ich eine berühmte Schauspielerin oder eine Prinzessin sein?'

No, it would be better to have new crayons or pretty earrings. Or maybe I want to be a famous actress or a princess?

Sie dachte daran, ihre Lieblingsbücher zu lesen mit ihren Freunden zu spielen. Sie dachte an Musik, Tanz und Malerei.

She thought of reading her favorite books and of playing with her friends. She thought of music, dancing and painting.

Sie dachte nach und dachte nach und dachte nach, aber sie wusste immer noch nicht, was sie wollte.
She thought and thought and thought, but she still didn't know what she wanted.

Sie dachte weiter nach, auch als ihr Vater von der Arbeit nach Hause kam. Wie jeden Abend spielten Amanda und ihr Vater Schach.
She carried on thinking even when her father came home from work. Just like every evening, Amanda and her father played chess.

Sie genoss das Schachspielen an diesem Abend so sehr, dass sie ihr Gespräch mit der Traumfee ganz vergaß.
She enjoyed playing chess that evening so much that she forgot all about her conversation with the dream fairy.

Als Amanda in dieser Nacht schlafen ging, hatte sie einen Traum.
That night when Amanda went to sleep, she had a dream.

In her dream, she walked through the doors of a big
building. She wandered down a long corridor, following
the sound of excited voices, until she entered a large
room.

It was a chess competition. She looked around and
heard her name called over the speakers. She was
going to play next!

In the first round, Amanda played against children of
her own age and won every single match. She was
excited, determined and surprisingly good at chess.

In the next round, she played against older children and
won every match again.

At the end of the day, she was titled the Chess
Champion.

Amanda wachte überglücklich auf. Der Traum hatte sich so echt angefühlt! Sie wollte eine Schachmeisterin werden. Sie nahm einen Stift, kritzelte „Schachmeisterin" auf ein Stück Papier und rannte aus ihrem Zimmer.

Amanda woke up overjoyed. The dream had felt so real! She wanted to be a chess champion. She picked up a pen, scribbled "chess champion" on a piece of paper and ran out of her room.

She hugged her father and shouted, "I'm going to be
a chess champion!"

Amanda's father smiled, gave her a tight hug and said,
"I believe in you, dear."

A few days passed and a chess competition was going
to be held at school. There was great excitement in the
air.

Amanda was nervous at first, but she was
confident she would win. After all, she had won the
championship in her dream.

From the moment the competition began, however, it
was obvious that Amanda wasn't as strong of a player
as she thought. She lost the very first game.

She was hurt and disappointed in herself. It wasn't
anything like the competition in her dream.

*Traurig und entmutigt kam Amanda nach Hause. Sie
setzte sich auf die Couch und fing an zu weinen.*
Sad and discouraged, Amanda arrived home. She sat
on the bed and started to cry.

„Wie konnte das passieren?", dachte sie. „Ich habe es doch so geträumt. Ich hätte gewinnen sollen!"
How could this happen? she thought. **I dreamed about this. I should have won!**

„Warum weinst du, Liebes?", sagte eine vertraute Stimme. Die Traumfee saß neben ihr.
"Why are you crying, dear?" said a familiar voice. The dream fairy was sitting next to her.

„Was nützt es, einen Traum zu haben, wenn er nicht wahr wird?", antwortete Amanda.
"What's the point in having a dream if it doesn't come true?" answered Amanda.

Die Traumfee legte ihren Arm um Amandas Schulter. „Damit dein Traum wahr wird, musst du üben", erklärte sie freundlich. „Du musst hart arbeiten und es immer und immer wieder versuchen, bis du ihn verwirklichst."
The dream fairy put her arm around Amanda's shoulder. "In order for your dream to come true, you have to practice," she explained kindly. "You have to work hard and try over and over again until you make it happen."

Amanda hörte der Traumfee aufmerksam zu und wusste, dass sie recht hatte.
Amanda listened carefully to the dream fairy and knew she was right.

„*Willst du wirklich, wirklich Schachmeisterin sein?*",
fragte die Fee.
"Do you really, really want to be a chess champion?"
asked the fairy.

„Mehr als alles andere auf der Welt." Amanda lächelte
und hörte auf zu weinen.
"More than anything else in the world." Amanda
smiled and stopped crying.

Die Traumfee rückte Amanda näher und flüsterte:
„Dann weißt du, was du tun solltest."
The dream fairy came closer to Amanda and
whispered, "Then you know what you should do."

Bevor Amanda noch ein Wort sagen konnte, verschwand die Fee.
Before Amanda could say another word, the fairy disappeared.

Amanda dachte einen Moment nach, sprang vom Bett und rannte zu ihrem Vater.
Amanda thought for a moment, hopped off the bed and ran to her father.

„Papa!", rief sie. „Ich will Schachmeisterin sein!"
"Dad!" she shouted. "I want to be a chess champion!"

„Ich weiß, Amanda, du hast es mir schon erzählt. Aber wie willst du das erreichen?", fragte er.
"I know, Amanda, you've already told me. But how are you going to accomplish it?" he asked.

„Ich möchte mich für einen Schachclub anmelden und ich werde jeden Tag üben. Ich will nicht einmal fernsehen oder mit meinen Spielzeugen spielen – ich will einfach nur das machen."
"I want to sign up for a chess club, and I'm going to practice every day. I don't even want to watch TV or play with my toys—I just want to do this."

„Bist du sicher?", fragte ihr Papa.
"Are you sure?" her dad asked.

„Ja!", antwortete Amanda. „Ich werde alles tun, um Schachmeisterin zu werden."
"Yes!" Amanda answered. "I will do anything to be the chess champion."

„Ich bin stolz auf dich, Schatz, ich weiß, dass du Erfolg haben wirst."
"I'm proud of you, sweetheart, I know you'll succeed."

Ihr Vater umarmte sie fest und Amandas Gesicht strahlte vor Stolz und Aufregung.
Her father hugged her tightly, and Amanda's face shone with pride and excitement.

Amanda begann für den nächsten Wettkampf zu trainieren. Sie verbrachte die meisten Tage damit, Schach zu spielen.
Amanda began to practice for the next competition. She spent most of her days playing chess.

Sie lernte im Schachclub, übte zuhause am Computer und spielte abends Schach mit ihrem Papa. Es störte sie nicht, nicht mit ihren Puppen zu spielen oder fernzusehen – sie war darauf konzentriert, die beste Schachspielerin zu werden, die sie sein konnte.
She studied at the chess club, practiced on the computer at home and played chess with her dad in the evenings. She didn't mind not playing with her dolls or watching TV—she was focused on becoming the best chess player she could be.

Finally, the day of the next competition arrived.
Amanda excitedly stood up for her first match and
met the same boy she had lost to in the previous
competition.

„Bist du bereit, wieder zu verlieren?", fragte der Junge spöttisch.
"Are you ready to lose again?" the boy asked mockingly.

Amanda lächelte nur. Tief in ihrem Herzen war sie überzeugt, dass sie bereit war.
Amanda just smiled. Deep in her heart, she was confident that she was ready.

Das Spiel begann sofort. Es war so einfach. Amanda gewann mit Leichtigkeit und freute sich darauf, mehr zu spielen.
The match began right away. Amanda won easily and was excited to play more.

Sie gewann das zweite, dritte und auch vierte Spiel und so ging es immer weiter. Jedes Spiel war schwerer als das Vorherige, aber dank ihrer harten Arbeit und Entschlossenheit gewann Amanda jedes Mal.
She won the second match, and the third and the fourth, and on it went. Each match was harder than the one before, but thanks to her hard work and determination, Amanda won every time.

Am Ende des Tages wurde Amanda der Titel
Schulschachmeisterin verliehen.
At the end of the day, Amanda was awarded the title
of School Chess Champion.

Sie zeigte ihre Medaille und Trophäe stolz ihrer Familie und ihren Freunden. Sie war so glücklich und wusste, dass sie alles erreichen konnte, was sie wollte.

She showed her medal and trophy proudly to her family and friends. She was so happy, and knew that she could achieve anything she wanted.

So fand Amanda ihren Traum und verwirklichte ihn.
That was how Amanda found her dream and made it come true.

Von diesem Tag an war Amanda nie wieder traurig. Sie weiß schon, was ihr nächster Traum sein wird und was sie tun muss, damit auch dieser in Erfüllung geht.
From that day on, Amanda was never sad again. Now she already knows what her next dream will be and what she has to do to make that one come true, too.

Was ist mit dir?
How about you?

Was ist dein Traum und was wirst du tun, damit er wahr wird?
What's your dream and what will you do to make it come true?